It's Harvest Time

It's Harvest Time

Reaping the Treasure God Has Waiting for You

Chandra Danner Livingston

iUniverse, Inc.
New York Lincoln Shanghai

It's Harvest Time
Reaping the Treasure God Has Waiting for You

All Rights Reserved © 2003 by Chandra Danner Livingston

No part of this book may be reproduced or transmitted in any form or by any means, graphic, electronic, or mechanical, including photocopying, recording, taping, or by any information storage retrieval system, without the written permission of the publisher.

iUniverse, Inc.

For information address:
iUniverse
2021 Pine Lake Road, Suite 100
Lincoln, NE 68512
www.iuniverse.com

ISBN: 0-595-28113-3

Printed in the United States of America

DEDICATION

To my wonderful husband, Rudy, and our darling children, Alysia, Emmanuel and Mia. Thank you for your loving support and for allowing Momma to spend so much time on the computer. When God blessed me with your love, "pleasure came into my life, chic."

To Carol and Lisa for your encouragement during the Wheeler Avenue Baptist Church women's retreat. To LaTricia, Bernadette, Birdia and Peggy…sincere thanks for lending your editing assistance. Your friendship is a treasure to me.

I would like to especially thank my prayer partners, Erica, Monique, Cheronda, Nikita, and Isabella. Thanks for keeping me "lifted up" during the wee hours of the morning. Thank you all for sharing your many talents with me.

Also, a heartfelt thanks goes to my mom and dad for always encouraging me. Your gifts of ministry are touching the lives of many people in the precious name of our Savior.

Contents

Preface ix

Chapter One Fertile Ground 1

Chapter Two Grow Where You Are Planted 4

Chapter Three "Whether" Conditions 13

Chapter Four Irrigating Your Fields 19

Chapter Five In Due Season 23

Chapter Six Labor Shortage 28

Chapter Seven Harvest Of Plenty 36

Preface

My Dear Friend,

Did you know that God has a treasure in heaven waiting for you to claim? Friends, a bountiful, sweet harvest of blessings awaits you, but you must nurture His Spirit from within to receive your spiritual earthly inheritance. I wish to share with you how to release the wonderful and awesome blessings God has set aside for each of us…blessings intended for our benefit during our earthly visitation.

Read on and discover how to begin to truly *LIVE*…

LIVE like a meadow stream, allowing your "stored" blessings to begin to flow through your life, nourishing all that it touches.

LIVE with a determination to "get it right"…living honestly before God and His People.

LIVE, allowing God's Word to serve as your instructional guide as you take life's journey.

NOW is the time to reap what God has in storage for you…
It's Harvest Time!

Chandra Danner Livingston

CHAPTER ONE

Fertile Ground

If you had the opportunity to tell your life story before a world audience, where would you begin? Maybe your childhood would be the logical place to start…or how about those exciting teen years? Or just maybe your career highlights would be where you would begin.

Unlike man, when our Almighty Creator chose to blueprint the details of Life itself, He began with *The Word*. "In the beginning was *The Word*, and *The Word* was with God, and *The Word* was God;" (St. John 1:1).

First impressions are important when it comes to making a lasting point and our Father wants to impress upon His children, first and foremost, the awesome, almighty power of *The Word*. It is *The Word* that formed the oceans, cast a million stars in the heavens and laid the foundation of the Earth. *The Word* formed man from Earth's dust into an image like His own.

Just think of it…God (*The Word*) used newly created, fertile soil to form the most highly engineered being to ever walk the face of the Earth! What began as mere dust, once scooped into the Master's hands, became fertile ground from which the Creator crafted humankind…dust transformed into fertile ground…by *The Word*.

It's *The Word* that made us, and *The Word* that keeps us. My friend, now ask yourself…is *The Word* still making me, molding me in His image? Or are the everyday cares of this world, "things" such as busy work schedules, financial issues, health concerns, s l o w l y turning me back into lifeless dust?

My beloved, the good news is that *God* (*The Word*) is still in the creation business! When David asked the Lord to…*"Create in me a clean heart, oh God, and renew a right spirit within me,"* (Psalms 51:10), he was asking, pleading in fact, for *The Word* to re-engineer him, everything about him, even his inner thoughts and spirit. Just as David was able to call on God in his hour of need, you too can call on the Lord and find help in times of trouble.

God is still in the Creation business.

Simply put, when you acknowledge and declare *The Word*, God answers! In fact, every question, problem, or concern that you will ever have has already been answered, and even documented for easy reference, in the Holy Bible. With this said, why then are we so ill-prepared when our so-called "issues" challenge our lives? Maybe it's because we're doing too much talking, and not enough listening?

Building Spiritual Rapport

Prayer is man's way of communicating with God. On the other hand, *The Word*, as chronicled in the Holy Scriptures, is God's way of communicating with humankind. With this in mind, ask yourself, "Am I doing all the talking in this relationship?" If so, then make it your goal, as a growing Christian, to maintain a spiritually balanced rapport with God. Rapport is defined as "relationship; especially one of mutual trust or emotional affinity." No relationship can flourish if one person is doing all the talking. God wants to build a lasting relationship with you…His Creation. He yearns to talk with you!

Therefore, strive to invest time with God. Simply put, as often as you can, *study* God's Word…attend Sunday school, Bible study, go on spiritual retreats…invest time in *The Word*. This is the best way to ensure that *The Word* (God) is allowed to minister (talk with you) on a consistent basis.

By carefully selecting study materials that are relevant to your "walk" (life with God on Earth), you will be assured that God's conversations with you will be nurturing and heartfelt because they will be specific to what's going on with you right now.

Hebrews 4:12 says, *"Indeed The Word of God is living and active, sharper than any two-edged sword, piercing until it divides soul from spirit, joints and marrow; it is able to judge the thoughts and intentions of the heart."* Freely translated, let God get a word in edgewise so He can freely operate in your life. Allow Him to examine your reasons for doing what you do. Once you allow yourself to bask in the marvelous light of God influenced living, you will begin to *Harvest the Treasure of Peace*.

Jewel: Philippians 4:7
And the Peace of God, which surpasses all understanding, will guard your hearts and your mind in Christ.

CHAPTER TWO

Grow Where You Are Planted

One of the things I love doing most is gardening. From soil preparation to planting and pruning, I enjoy it all. But it hasn't always been that way. When I first began gardening, all I wanted was immediate results, at any price I might add.

For instance, I once purchased very select, full-grown begonias to plant in my front yard, right next to the front porch. In a hurry to get it done, I didn't properly prepare my flowerbeds. I just planted. Well, you can imagine what happened. Not even a week had passed before they all but fell dead. After a brief investigation, I was "introduced" to the culprit…gumbo soil.

Gumbo soil (according to my neighbor who, by the way, has a gorgeous yard) is *not* what you want in your flowerbed. It is rock hard when dry, and gooey like paste when wet. In fact, gumbo soil is great material for bricks, not begonias.

Well, you best believe I now start with the soil for it's the soil that holds the nutrients needed to support plant life. These nutrients, once absorbed in the plant's root system, sustain the very life and beauty of the plant.

And so it is with our spiritual life. It's not just the outer display that counts. True spirituality comes from within, emerging from a soul nurtured by the Holy Spirit.

True Or Faux

In my quest to constantly improve my garden, I often drive around my neighborhood admiring other landscapes and making notes for future projects. I once remember driving by a yard that was absolutely stunning! In fact, this yard was so gorgeous that I stopped the car to get out and take a closer look.

As I approached the first flowerbed and leaned over for a closer inspection, I soon learned that all the flowers were fake! No wonder they looked so perfect; they were made of plastic! Obviously, the owner simply chose to "go through the motions" of gardening.

Quite often, we too find ourselves just "going through the motions" of Christianity. We attend church, but The Church is not in us. We pray memorized, ritualistic prayers, but never really have a "heart to heart" talk with the Father. However, true Christian living is about being "for real," genuine, and true to the Faith; not fake or faux. It's not enough to just look good. We should be truly striving, yearning, and hoping for a life rich in Godly (God focused) deeds (I Timothy 6:18).

Christian living is about being for real...genuine...true to the Faith, not fake or faux.

The Bible also cautions us in II Timothy 3:5 about having "the outward form of Godliness, but denying (not allowing) the power therein." In other words, like a flower denied access to the sun, by not living a genuine Christian life, we cut off vital spiritual nutrients needed for our lives to flourish and produce. Remember, it is through the power (inner vitality) of the Holy Spirit that we truly grow and blossom into mature Christians, producing much fruit. Now the key to obtaining your spiritual fruit is to go ahead and *decide to grow*.

For example, when gardeners finally decide to get serious about gardening, they add fertilizer and other vital nutrients to spark abundant plant growth. You too must spark your growth with an inward desire to become a better you. Right now, at this very moment, make up your mind to *grow where you are planted*. No matter where you are in your spiritual growth, baby Christian or maturing believer, make a pledge to yourself, right where you are, to accelerate your spiritual growth and never stop growing! Constant, uninterrupted growth allows your life to ripen on The Vine.

The Vine-Ripened Life

Have you ever tasted a vine-ripened tomato? Unlike store-ripened tomatoes, vine-ripened tomatoes are rich in color, slightly sweet, and more succulent. Your life will also become sweeter and more abundant as you absorb passages of scripture that hold the key to fruit-filled living. Just continue to stay attached to The Vine by studying *The Word*.

Remember Jesus' words in St. John 15:5: "*I am the vine, you are the branches. Those who abide in me, and I in them, bear much fruit, because apart from me you can do nothing.*" In this passage, Jesus shares the secret of spiritual growth, and that is to stay attached to Him (The Vine). My friends, just stay close to Jesus; study His words and His ways. Become familiar with His boyhood as well as His adult ministry; absorb it all!

One way to begin to know Him better is to reserve a portion of your personal time for Christian fellowship at various levels. Some examples include:

- Home study of the Bible
- Christian reference books and tapes
- Sunday School and other formal study groups
- Christian retreats, seminars, and workshops
- Early morning prayer and meditation
- Sharing your faith with others
- Passing down your faith legacy to your children
- Praising God as though nobody's watching you, but Him

Fellowship experiences are the key to an abundant, fruit-filled life.

Spiritual growth can also be experienced in a casual "grassroots" setting, such as a monthly inspirational book club meeting, or a friendly get-together with neighbors. With just a little research and creativity on your part, you will find that there are numerous ways to bolster your success at Christian living. Simply commit to spending quality time with the Lord each day. By investing (planting) time each day in cultivating your relationship with Jesus Christ (The Vine), you *will* begin to prosper (mature). Simply allow your daily tasks, thoughts, and deeds to be a reflection of a life yielded to Christ. Soon you too, like a tree planted by the river, will develop a deep-rooted faith that keeps you steady in the storm, and basking in the Son. Just think of it; no matter what the day brings, no matter what life throws your way, just by being "connected" to The Vine, you will begin to *Harvest the Treasure of Fruit-filled Living.*

> **Jewel: Psalms 1:3**
> They are like trees planted by streams of water, which yield their fruit in its season, and their leaves do not wither. In all that they do, they prosper.

Once your life begins to bear fruit, make an effort to "keep your plant maintenance up." In other words, continue growing your relationship with the Lord. Don't let up until your faith is deeply rooted, or you may end up not appreciating the very things that are designed to bless your life. Here's an example of what I mean.

Kid Crazy

Everybody gets a little "crazy" now and then, even the best of us. Like most well-intentioned Christian parents, when I find myself "over the edge" with my kids, I promise God that I will never "go there" again. Then, before you know it, there I am again, back in my "old skin:" angry, stressed, agitated, restless, useless, etc…(you get the picture). And even worse, it seems to come out of nowhere!

There I am again, back in my "old skin".

I remember a time when the kids were all piled up, as usual, in the "parents' only" bed one evening, watching television. We were waiting for the opening ceremony of the 2002 Winter Olympics to come on. Earlier, the kids were engaged in their usual winter sport (their favorite sport in fact), the "stomach tickle." Quite naturally, my son was the usual target of my two daughters. All while they were tickling him, he pleaded for relief. However, I *tuned them out* and instead kept my eyes on the television. After all, this event only comes on once every four years! Finally, the opening ceremony began and the girls and I settled in under the warm bed blanket to watch this international winter spectacle unfold.

Suddenly, my son decides to "take his revenge" by playfully leaping high into the air and landing solidly on my oldest daughter's back! Well, she immediately screeched in pain. After checking to see if she was OK, I lashed out at him, explaining how awful a thing that was for him to do to his sister. I really let him have it, going on and on about how much bigger and stronger he was than his sisters and that he should be careful not to play so rough with them. I repeated my rule, at the top of my voice I might add, that he was not to practice his "football moves" on his sisters. "Save all that for the football field," I said, finger-pointing.

All the while, my son was desperately trying to explain that he was "just playing," just as they had been playing with him earlier, "tickling him to death," as he put it. Clearly, I thought, he just "doesn't get it" and besides, all this fuss was causing me to miss the Olympics!

Clearly he just "doesn't get it."

Exhausted by it all, I just sent him straight to bed, not giving him a chance to explain his point of view. Crushed, he stormed into his room and closed the door. Later that evening, my husband brought the whole scene back up again, emphasizing the fact that I didn't say anything when the girls were tickling him non-stop. "Tickling and tackling are not the same thing," I replied. To which my husband wisely responded, "but to our son, tackling is playing."

Later on, I thought about it and my husband was indeed right. Even though his style of playing tends to be more zealous than the girls due to his larger size, in his mind, he's just playing. With that said, I gathered my courage and went straightway to my son's room to apologize. Luckily, he was still awake.

Simply put, he had been "wounded."

I began by telling him how sorry I was for not seeing his side of the story and that Momma was sorry for yelling at him. However, he didn't want to hear it. No matter how hard I tried, he wouldn't accept my apology. Simply put, he had been wounded by the one person on Earth designed to nurture him, not *nag* him, into correct living.

After numerous attempts to make things right between us, my son finally said, "Mom, just forget it; you can leave my room now." At that moment, deep sadness and regret overwhelmed me. "How did it all come to this?" I wondered.

Early the next morning, I quietly entered his room and stood next to his bed (he was in the top bunk). As I stood there, I reflected on all of the wonderful things about him…feeling so fortunate and blessed that he was *my* son. All of the sudden, he slowly began to wake up. "What should I say?" I wondered. "How should I begin?"

I reflected on all of the wonderful things about him…feeling so fortunate and blessed that he was my son.

I decided to try to make him laugh as he woke up by doing something funny, so I puckered my lips really, really big and just stood there as he focused his sleepy eyes on my face. Realizing what I was doing, he smiled and then planted a big "smooch" on my cheek. And with that, (and a couple of "big Momma" hugs) all was forgiven.

Later on, after he had gotten up and dressed, I apologized again and this time, he gladly accepted it. I now realize that children are a precious gift from God and should be cherished and nurtured at all times.

Children are a precious gift from God.

As you can see, I had a few stubborn wrinkles in "my old skin." Meekness and temperance were not my strong suit at that time in my life. Eventually, I had to find a way to "cure my madness." I knew I had to figure out a way to remain attached to The Vine to *truly* continue growing in Christ, but how?

Curing My Madness

Well, after much prayer and study, I learned that to cure *my madness*, I had to focus on bible lessons that featured scriptures that teach self-control and temperament. The key word here is "focus."

Think of it like this. Just as a medical doctor thoroughly examines a patient to determine the appropriate medical treatment, your God, the Good Physician, has a Word for whatever ails you. However, it is our job to "take the right medicine." In other words, we must obey and live according to the scriptures that specifically address our weaknesses and sinful tendencies in order to be delivered from them. For example, if your problem is jealously, a lesson on say…overeating…may not be the "medicine" for that particular condition of the heart. To overcome an emotion as strong as jealously takes real work. Basically, you must search the Bible for scriptures that specifically deal with jealously and envy. Then, constantly study and meditate on these scriptures until they become so familiar to you that you apply them at just the right moment. Remember, *it is the application of God's word that transforms you from a hearer of the Word into a doer of the Word (James 1:22).*

Finally, pray to the Father for sustained deliverance. What I mean by this is that once you are delivered, don't stop there. Resolve next to routinely evaluate and examine yourself.

Take time out to make an honest assessment of your faults so you'll know, and deal with, the real truth about you. Then study God's word in these specific areas to remain free from the bondage of these sins. By developing and maintaining a "focused" study of God's word, you will begin to *Harvest the Treasure of Freedom.*

> **Jewel: II Corinthians 3:17**
>
> *Now the Lord is that Spirit: and where the Spirit of the Lord is, there is freedom.*

CHAPTER THREE

"Whether" Conditions

I often take inventory of all the stuff I have around the house. You know, the unused gadgets in the kid's toy box, my bedroom closet, the laundry room; all the usual places that seem to attract items that are no longer useful but too nice to just throw away. When deciding whether to keep an item or just throw it out, I try to determine if it has a future benefit. I  ask myself, "Do I really need an egg-shaped Jell-O mold…do I even have time to make dessert anyway?" Whether to keep or cast, save or discard, the decision always seems to revolve around what I call "whether" conditions.

Every "thing" deserves utility…a place of service.

"Whether" conditions are simply future circumstances that will cause me to need an item later on. For instance, "whether" it has any sort of future benefit as a part of a school project, or "whether" my husband can salvage parts from it for his next household repair.

Whatever reasons I can come up with to justify holding on to an item are what I call my "whether" conditions. Usually, there are so many

13

unknowns, yet one thing's for sure: just taking up space, collecting dust is *not* an option. Every "thing" deserves utility, usefulness; a place of service.

Hmmm...wouldn't it be nice if we all found our rightful place...our "spot"...our role in the spiritual realm? Ask yourself, "Am I collecting dust, saving myself for some unknown future use, or am I actively serving God now? What really is my purpose, utility or earthly mission?"

My Mission

When you think of the word "mission," what comes to mind? Purpose...Duty...Required Task? How about the word beauty? Yes, *beauty*! I know it may seem like an odd word to associate with mission, but consider this. Psalm 90:17 says, *"And let the beauty of the Lord our God be upon us: and establish thou the work of our hands upon us; yea, the work of our hands establish thou it."*

God's beauty is upon those who are working for Him.

Simply put, God's beauty is upon those who are working for Him, whose daily tasks are established (motivated) by His word. Therefore, it's no great mystery as to what we as Christians should be doing, yet how often do we hear ourselves say, "Oh, I just don't know what God has called me to do; I'm just not sure what I should be doing."

My friend, our mission, our great commission, is to share the gospel of Jesus Christ and to spread the good news of salvation. Matthew 28:19 says, *"Go ye therefore and teach all nations, baptizing them in the name of the Father, the Son and the Holy Spirit."* Now, **how you carry that mission out is mostly up to you!**

Some of us will be assigned to foreign mission fields, while others will have a more domestic task of evangelizing in our local neighborhoods. Others will have more formal roles in local churches, such as ministers,

Sunday school teachers, and counselors. Still others will be assigned to the streets, serving the homeless, runaway teens or those addicted to drugs. Whatever "form" your mission takes is up to you. But be assured that the basic goal of every Christian's mission is to simply share the Gospel of Jesus Christ.

So stop saying, "I don't know what God wants me to do." Yes, you do know; we all know, for we all have the same assignment, the same mission, and the same goal. We are to seek and to save; that's it! Therefore, the real question, my friend, is not *what* your mission is, but *when* and *how will you carry it out*?

What's Hindering Me?

With all the cares of this world closing in on us day by day, you may wonder if you will ever begin carrying out your mission. You may be thinking, "I barely have enough strength to figure out how to manage my own life, let alone be an example for some other poor soul!" My friend, please know that God is fully aware of your limitations. So rest assured that you're not expected, nor have you been designed, to actually *do* the saving. We are just sowers. We simply are to plant God's word into the minds of those who will hear. We do that through our personal testimony, our life example, or maybe even through our written thoughts.

Remember, God designed the blueprint for humankind. Thus, He knows our areas of weakness as well as our amazing strengths and talents. We are only asked to plant the seed of faith; share His Word, His Love and His Light. Psalms 55:22 says, *"Turn your worries over to the Lord. He will keep you going. He will never let godly people fall."* So you see, we are just to allow Him to keep us going. Then as we journey, we simply keep planting

He knows our areas of weakness as well as our amazing strengths and talents.

the seeds of faith, whenever and wherever we can. Then God, and only God, will give the increase (I Corinthians 3:6).

No matter what method you use, simply speak and demonstrate His Word in your life. His Word, once received, will then begin to transform the hearts and minds of your "hearers." God just wants us to be the willing helpers He can use to transform (transition from death to life) those around us. This transformation is the ultimate indication of our fulfillment of *the* mission. Now, once you "find your spot," *doing* what you're supposed to be doing, you will then begin to *Harvest the Treasure of the Wise Steward*.

Jewel: Luke 12:42 & 43

And the Lord said, who then is the faithful and wise steward, whom his master will set over his household, to give them their portion of food at the proper time? Blessed is that servant who his master when he comes will find so doing.

Mission *Possible*

Have you ever wondered how is it possible that God can take our lives, just at the right moment, and use it to carry out His mission? How is it that He knows where to place us when we are needed, in just the right spot, equipped with everything we need for that moment?

The truth is, God is all-powerful and uses His power to empower us to serve. However, this attitude of service does not naturally come to us. It is an attitude that evolves as we spend time with the Father.

Yet, so often, we find ourselves just waiting for the right moment to serve, the right time and place, the perfect situation in our lives before we find utility in the Kingdom. The truth is, *there is no perfect time, place or situation…no ideal moment to begin.*

The truth is, God is all-powerful and uses His power to empower us to serve.

All you need to do is *just decide to be useful.* Let me make myself clear on this one. In other words, just *being available* for use is not good enough. Saying things like, "Lord, just let me know what you want me to do," is not a statement that genuinely suggests our willingness to serve. That's like saying, "Hey, I'm free Lord; just let me know *if* you need my participation."

Now, let's be "for real!" God has already informed us that it's His will for us to be active members of the family of God. James 1:22 says, *"Don't just listen to the Word. You fool yourselves if you do that. You must do what it says."*

God wants us to always actively seek where we can be of service to Him. Simply begin to think of yourself as a local missionary. Whether it's working with wayward youth, assisting an elderly couple with their weekly errands, witnessing to those who have lost their way, or just being good parents, no matter what the mission field, look beyond your personal circumstances and seek to have usefulness in Christ.

Believe me, finding your place in Christ is a good thing, for I have found that usefulness brings about deep, personal satisfaction within my soul. Just knowing I'm in His will, seems to quiet all the "noise" of life.

What "noise" am I speaking of? Well, I define this "noise" as any negative thoughts I wish not to hear, receive, accept, or invite into my mind or spirit. As a growing Christian, the "self-doubt" noise, "worried and anxious noise, lies from the enemy" noise, and any other situation that causes me to feel that I am unfit for service to God, I just toss those thoughts aside, and so should you.

Besides, keep in mind that none of us are perfect. We all have "issues," but that's OK. My friend, it's *not* an issue-free life that God requires, but a life that will serve Him and trust Him to resolve our issues, *while* we are serving Him.

Keep in mind that none of us are perfect.

Therefore, "whether" you are poor or rich, "whether" equipped or stripped, "whether" you have arrived, or barely alive; no matter what your "whether conditions" are, if you love God, you have a duty to find usefulness in Christ. So begin to just serve Him, where you are, no matter what condition your life is in. Allow yourself to be an active Kingdom builder, and soon you will find that your "whether conditions" don't matter at all! Once you take your rightful place in service to God, you will begin to *Harvest the Treasure of Assurance.*

> **Jewel: Isaiah 32:17**
> And the effect of righteousness will be peace, and the result of righteousness, quietness and assurance forever.

Chapter Four

Irrigating Your Fields

Oh, the glories of water! It quenches our thirst, cleans and nourishes our bodies, and even revives our souls. Yes, our very souls are served by water…the Living Water. Just as thirsty fields are routinely bathed in life-  giving water, so must our souls (our attitudes, emotions, motives, our entire "thought life"), must be flooded with the living water (God's Word) in order for our lives to flourish and grow.

However, this living, life-giving water needs a reservoir, a place of storage and containment—a vessel. God's vessel of choice, my friends, is your mind.

God's vessel of choice, my friends, is your mind.

Jeremiah 31:33b says, "*I will put my law* (the living water) *in their minds. I will write it on their hearts. I will be their God, and they shall be my people.*" God's laws are intended to guide us into righteous living. By keeping His laws, we are assured a freedom-filled life. But to be a law-keeper, we must first know the lawgiver. We must know that He has our best interests at heart and that His law is intended to bless us and carry us through.

We must also realize that His law is based in Love and is always meant for our ultimate good. So if the law is "all good," why not choose to transform yourself into a law-abiding vessel? Simply decide to start each day by getting to know God first. Make Him a priority by putting Him at the top of your list.

Blessed Morning

Let me suggest that you begin your mornings with God. In the peaceful quiet of early morning, just before the break of dawn, take a few moments to focus and concentrate your mind totally, without distraction of any kind, on God. Psalm 5:3 says, *"Lord, in the morning you hear my voice. In the morning I pray to you. I wait for you in hope."*

Reserve a quiet "meeting spot";
A place in your home set aside where you can meet with God face to face.

Reserve a quiet "meeting spot"—a place in your home set aside where you can meet with God face-to-face. Begin your meeting with honest, real conversation. Genuinely express yourself, your gratitude, your praise, your hopes and your dreams. Also share the parch places with Him as well…your doubts, your fears, your concerns. Just allow yourself to be fully exposed, discussing in prayer the good as well as the not-so-good. Once all of these thoughts have been released and shared, replace them with God's thoughts.

To do this, simply open your Bible and begin to read scriptures that affirm God as your Deliverer, your Peace and your Comforter. Allow these scriptures to flood your mind with Godly thinking. Isaiah 55:9 says, *"For as the heavens are higher than the Earth, so are my ways higher than your ways, and my thoughts than your thoughts."* Isaiah 55:11 promises, *"So shall my word be that goeth forth out of my mouth: it shall not return unto me void, but it shall accomplish that which I please, and it shall prosper in the thing whereto I sent it."* Simply put, allow God's promises to raise you above your circumstances. You can count on Him to keep His word. It's all a matter of how you choose to view your life.

Through The Eyes Of Love

Instead of focusing on a negative view of your life, filter your way of thinking through God's Word. The bottom line is God loves you, *all* of you, even the parts of you that still need a lot of work! So you might as well change the way you view yourself as someone who is lovingly cherished by the Almighty. With this thought in mind, strive to envision God's perspective.

Begin to view yourself as someone who is lovingly cherished by the Almighty.

Just think on these things…

- God Is never surprised by what you do

    (John 4:29)

- God Knows the outcome…He has already worked it out

    (Isaiah 65:24)

- God Knows what He's doing…He wants you to trust His competence

    (Proverbs 3:26)

- God Knows about *all* your tomorrows…Trust Him with your future

    (Proverbs 2: 8-10)

- God Knows the best route…He desires to lead you

    (St. John 10: 27 & 28)

- God Is always aware of your suffering

    (Psalm 31:7)

- God Knows all the details…He is preparing a schedule for you

    (Jeremiah 29:11)

My friend, God knows…He *really* knows, and sees, and cares. Nothing escapes His notice, so begin daily to consciously think like He thinks, and then respond to life how He would respond. Irrigate your thoughts with the Living Water of God's word by thinking about what God wants you to think about. Allow the *Living Water* to float your cares away!

Philippians 4:8 says, "*Finally, my brothers and sisters, always think about what is true. Think about what is noble, right and pure. Think about what is lovely and worthy of respect. If anything is excellent or worthy of praise, think about those kinds of things.*"

By transforming your mind into a vessel that is daily flooded with Godly thinking, you will begin to *Harvest the Treasure of Wisdom*.

Jewel: Proverbs 4:7
Wisdom is best. So get wisdom. No matter what it costs, get understanding.

Chapter Five

In Due Season

We all transverse this life through various seasons…times of joy and sorrow, love and hate. As with any season, these moments in time are never permanent; they all have an allotted space, an appointed time.

Quite possibly, you've heard your mother say, "There is a time and place for everything, and now is *not* the time." If you're like me, you may have wondered, "Will it *ever* be *my* time?"

Now is the time to listen to your Father.

Well, now is the time to listen to your Father. He has a heavenly "organizer" and believe me—you're in it! Your failures, your successes, your near misses, as well as the times when you get it just right—these "seasons"—are all there, meticulously chartered, synchronized and monitored by God.

Ecclesiastes Chapter 3, Verses 1 through 8, states: *"There is a time for everything. There's a time for everything that is done on Earth. There is a time to be born. And there's a time to die. There is a time to plant. And*

23

there's a time to pull up what is planted. There is a time to kill. And there's a time to heal. There is a time to tear down. And there's a time to build up. There is a time to cry. And there's a time to laugh. There is a time to be sad. And there's a time to dance. There is a time to scatter stones. And there's a time to gather them. There is a time to hug. And there's a time not to hug. There is a time to search. And there's a time to stop searching. There is a time to keep. And there's a time to throw away. There is a time to tear. And there's a time to mend. There is a time to be silent. And there is a time to speak. There is a time to love. And there's a time to hate. There is a time for war. And there is a time for peace."

And so it is. God, in His infinite wisdom has already authored our timeline in His "personal planner" through which our lives are set to Divine Order. He knows when and where every circumstance in your life will take place; when you will marry, when you move back home; when you will prosper and when you will be in need…it's all there. Remember that God is organized. (He created every living thing in just seven days…you can't get more organized than that!)

Remember… God is organized.

He knows the number of hairs on your head, even the exact amount of sand on every shore. Nothing happens without His knowledge, because it's all documented in His plan. So you see, it's futile to become frustrated when things don't happen when you want them to.

Instead, realize that you have an appointment with destiny. In other words, everything that's going to happen will happen in God's time, the appointed time; not your time, but His. Whether you like it or not—God's timetable rules. So the wise thing to do is to align your schedule with the Master's plan.

The Master's Plan

God has a plan and a purpose for you. In fact, His plan is "tailor-made," because He already knows about your successes and failures before they even happen. Also, His plan is designed to bless *you, in spite of you.* So, what are you waiting for! Now is the time to stay focused, stay true, stay hopeful, and stay in the race (Hebrews 12:1).

Be determined to stick with the master plan and don't get tired of "doing the right thing." Let me assure you that righteous living *always* pays off! By doing what is right, the Father will continue to prepare a time and place for you. He will give you a divine appointment for every situation that will occur in your life. Now ask yourself, am I willing to keep all my appointments with God?

You're Not On My Books

I remember vividly last year a time when I just couldn't seem to keep my hair appointments straight in my mind. I would arrive on a day I *thought* I had an appointment, only to hear "you're not on my books." I must admit it was during a time when I was *way* too busy. I had a work project that took me 50 miles on the other side of town most of the week. I also had my church work and my mom work...the kids, the husband and the house. I had so many things to do in such a small space of time, so it seemed. Yet, when I look back, it really was a matter of doing a better job of staying "balanced." Basically, I can't let one task unfairly crowd out another.

So I began to better organize my calendar, being sure that my appointments were all documented. I also made sure that each appointment was appropriately spaced apart to assure their completion. I figured, why should I schedule my appointments so close together, knowing the odds are that I probably won't have time to make it? So, I stopped that practice. Instead, I began to plan and allow time for the "in-between time" (the meantime) with the same care as I had planned my appointments.

In The Interim...

God allows for interim or "meantimes" as well…those moments of rest and recovery between our seasons. Yet, we often don't get a chance to enjoy the wonderful schedule He has put together, because we choose to *not* follow His will for our lives. We are sure that our agenda is far more relevant and important than His. Our priorities make perfect sense to us, so we feverishly attempt to "make it happen." Yet, "It ain't *hap'nen,* and we still don't get it." My friend, the only way to stay in balance is to follow the Master's plan; the best blueprint for our lives!

Meanwhile…"Back at the Ranch"

Meanwhile, God is hoping, longing for His children to come back into the fold, to join His "posse".

Meanwhile, all the time you are trying to do it on your own, God is hoping, longing for His children to come back into the fold, to join His "posse" back at the ranch. In Jeremiah 29:11, God declares, *"I know the plans I have for you, announces the Lord. I want you to enjoy success. I do not plan to harm you. I will give you hope for the years to come."* So you see, He's already "figured it out, worked you in and hooked you up!" Now is the time to stay on His schedule, swap your plans for His, and stay on His books…all 66 of them! With God, all your "seasons" and divine appointments for your life will happen at the appropriate time, God's time. No matter what you've already "worked out in your head," God's plan is the best plan for you because He does everything decently and in order (I Corinthians 14:40).

He allows for the sweet times, the lean times, and all the meantimes in between to have a clear purpose for occurring. Each moment of your life is designed to nurture and *grow* you...*show* you just how dependable He is! His plan is also perfectly balanced to allow *all* your experiences...your joys as well as your sorrows...to make *you a better you!*

So begin to realize that season-by-season, moment-by-moment, every circumstance is designed to lead you closer to Him. And in His presence is where abundant life is found. In His plan, there's ample time on the schedule to "smell the roses" as well as "make the bacon." My dear friend, by turning your daily schedule over to God, you will most assuredly begin to *Harvest the Treasure of Daily Benefits.*

> **Jewel: Psalm 68:19**
> Blessed be the Lord who daily loadeth us with benefits, even the God of our Salvation.

CHAPTER SIX

Labor Shortage

Right now, at this very moment, take an assessment of your *physical* state. Are your tired, listless and out of energy? Do you detect a gnawing pain in your lower back...or even worse, does your neck seem to have a permanent crook in it? (Ouch!) And how about your mental state...is it suffering too?

Do you know how important it is to care for your total body, your temple?

Well, you are not alone. Just think for a moment about the response you got the last time you casually asked a friend, "How's it going?" You likely heard something like "Oh...(deep sigh) it's *Going*." Or, "I could use a nap right about now." The glaring truth seems to be that we are all constantly *Going, Doing, Being, Working, and Driving Ourselves Into The Ground!*

Just think about it. We eat foods that virtually have all the nutrients processed out of them. We don't get enough rest, drink enough water, get enough exercise, and on top of that, we don't even spend enough time with those we love. Well, *enough is enough!*

Time to Get Serious

Do you know how important it is to care for your total *body—your temple*? It's important if we are to be effective laborers for Christ. But how can we be laborers for the Lord when we don't have the strength to get out of bed most mornings?

Maybe our lack of physical care is the main reason there seems to be a Christian labor shortage. In fact, I have found in my own life that a weary mind and body quickly falls prey to the sin of spiritual laziness. Simply put, without physical stamina, you will find it very difficult to focus on spiritual things. However, it is God's desire for you to be in total health, both in mind and body.

The Mind/Body Connection

You are not just a one-dimensional physical entity. You also have a spiritual side. *Both need to workout.* Physical and spiritual health goes hand in hand as one-dimension nurtures the other. You should realize that without proper care of *The Body of* ____*(your name)*____, you won't maintain the physical endurance and sustaining energy needed to *really* live life.

But did you also realize that without the proper care of *The Body of Christ, The Church* (God's People) will not have the mental focus to produce what I like to refer to as our "spiritual dividends," our Fruit. Our Fruit, as mentioned in Galatians 5:22, consists of love, joy, peace, patience, kindness, generosity, faithfulness, gentleness and self-control. These spiritual attributes are more easily attained when your physical health develops in concert with your spiritual growth. Therefore, make a collaborative effort to join body and soul in a spiritual bond toward *total* health.

Get Moving!

By now, we all "know the drill" about our physical health. What we need to do now is simply *make the time to get serious and get moving!* Now, how you decide to move is up to you...

Walk   Run
      Hike   Bike
           Lift   Climb
                 Bend   Stretch
                       Step   Glide   Ride...

Just choose any physical activity that works well with your spirit, your personality and your lifestyle. There are tons of material on the proper care of the body, so you won't have a problem finding the information you need. Just be careful to do your homework and choose a routine that is *customized to you*, so you'll stick with it!

Got Milk?

Now I know this "get physical stuff" isn't anything you haven't heard before. With that in mind, why then do we sometimes "slack off" when it comes to maintaining our physical health? Maybe, we don't have what it takes.

Ever wonder what does it take to really get serious about our health...serious enough to cherish and nurture our bodies on a consistent basis? The key is to come to the realization that a healthier body serves to equip, enable, prepare and sustain us for spiritual battle.

> The key is to come to the realization that a healthier body serves to equip, enable, prepare, and sustain us for spiritual battle.

It's not just about looking good and feeling good, but also about *being* good and faithful servants in God's Kingdom! When we realize that the degree of our physical stamina determines our ability to "fight the good fight," we should then develop the proper motive to "just do it," and keep doing it!

And as you're "doing it," don't forget to intake the spiritual nutrients only found in God's Word. That's *the real "milk" for life!*

1 Peter 2:2 says, *"Like babies that were just born, you should long for the pure milk of God's word. It will help you grow up as believers."* So you see, it takes spiritual milk to nurture our "backbone" (that dogmatic determination to live for Christ)!

So workout, study and pray! Pray for the will to maintain your physical state to be of maximum service for Him. Right now, decide to just take better care of yourself and your family. Sure, it takes a little more effort to prepare a home-cooked meal versus heating up a frozen dinner in the microwave, but your body is worth the sacrifice of your time. Roman 12:1 speaks of *"presenting your bodies as a living sacrifice, holy and acceptable to God, which is your spiritual worship."* Just think about it. Taking proper care of our bodies is a part of our worship!

So live in such a way that maximizes your potential to worship God! In order to live right, we must move right, eat right and sleep right. When we "keep on keeping on" in service to God, we will soon enjoy the benefits of a mutually healthy body and soul. Staying committed to maintaining your Temple in good working order will allow you to *Harvest the Treasure of Prospering Health.*

Jewel: John III 2
Beloved, I wish above all things that thou mayest prosper and be in health, even as thy soul prospereth.

And Still I (High) Rise

The best time for me to workout is in the morning, right after I finish my prayer time. I must admit that I'm not as consistent as I would like to be, but I'm getting better. I try not to limit myself to a set routine, but instead try to get some sort of physical movement in each day. A few years ago, I even asked my husband to buy me a workout mat for Christmas. I figured after years of neglect, the *floor* would be the best place to start. My ultimate goal is to build up my stamina so I can easily descend the stairs at work if I ever need to. This would be no small feat as my office is located in a high-rise building in Texas, many stories above street level.

For me, every time I take the elevator in my building is an act of faith, especially considering the events of September the 11th. In my building, the elevator carefully paces itself to each floor. I use this time to affirm Jude 1:24 and 25 which says, "*Now unto Him that is able to keep you from falling, and to present you faultless before the presence of His Glory with exceeding joy, to the only wise God our Savior, be glory and majesty, dominion and power, both now and ever. Amen.*" With that meditation said, I'm good to go.

Besides, I am blessed to have a wonderful job working for an organization that provides assistance to local charities. What a joy it is for me to have such meaningful labor! I've only been on staff a short while, but so far, so good, and then *it* happened.

Is This A Drill?

One Friday, during the late morning hours, I was busy working on a report when a piercing emergency siren broke the usual serenity of our Houston office. Startled, I immediately stood up and began to wonder, *is this a drill?* Then over the public speakers came a very loud voice. It was building personnel instructing us to go immediately to the stairwell and await further instructions. Instantly, I grabbed my emergency gear, which consisted of an old diaper (to prevent smoke inhalation) and a flashlight. I also grabbed my fake, battery operated night-vision gargles. I borrowed the gargles from my son who thought they might come in handy one day. A mere toy, certainly, and when I strapped them on, I was the source of humor for the entire office now gathered at the stairway. I too thought they were funny looking, but at that moment, I just grabbed everything.

Equipped and anxious, we all stood there for what seemed like forever, constantly listening to the building personnel repeat the same directions over and over; "Go to the stairwell and await instructions." Well, let me tell you, just waiting in a high-rise during an emergency situation is not an easy task. I must admit a few of us were contemplating taking the stairs, yet we did as we were instructed, patiently hoping that our obedience would somehow benefit us in the end.

Finally, a security officer came to our floor and told us to evacuate four floors down, where we would then receive further instructions. At that point, we were sure this wasn't a drill. Hurriedly, we all proceeded to a small elevator designed to hold eight or nine people comfortably. However, wanting to stay together, all 15 or so of us piled in. I used this time in the elevator to jokingly let our president know that I would be happy to buy everyone a pair of my fake night-vision gargles…"only six bucks a shot," I quipped. I've always had a quick wit that usually serves to bring smiles to the faces around me; this time was no exception. Besides, it kept me from thinking about what was really going on.

Once we reached our destination, we were given the OK to continue down to the lobby at street level. After the elevator doors closed again, I instinctively began to recite my scripture as usual, but this time, I turned to my boss and recited the scripture audibly, as though we were having a conversation. Afterwards, she and I exchanged warm smiles, as we often do. Once we reached the ground floor, we learned that an elevator motor had burned out on the floor right below our offices, causing smoke to pour from that elevator into the hallway. Wow! Had we not followed the orders we were given, we might have run right into the danger we were trying to avoid! It's a good thing we chose to follow instructions.

That's all God wants us to do…just follow instructions. Yet so many times, we choose to venture out on our own, not trusting the One who really knows what's going on; yet all God wants is for us to trust His competence. Believe it or not, God really is smarter than you! He knows what He's doing; all you need to do is just trust and depend on Him. Isaiah 55:9 says, *"For as the heavens are higher than the Earth, so are my ways higher than your ways, and my thoughts than your thoughts."* Thus, our brainpower is no match for the Omniscience of God. God's word in Joshua 1:8 says, *"This book of the law shall not depart out of thy mouth, but thou shalt mediate therein day and night, that thou mayest observe to do according to all that is written therein: for then thou shalt make thy way prosperous, and then thou shalt have good success."*

All Clear

Later on after the upper floors were inspected and determined to be safe for occupation, we were given the go ahead to go back up to our floor. Once I returned to my office, I decided to do something that would not require me to have to concentrate too much, considering all the drama that had happened earlier. For me, that would be filing.

As I began to sort and collate what must have been hundreds of letters, reports and brochures, I found it easier to form piles by calendar year. Soon I had large piles for 2000, 2001 and 2002. Once in a while, a memo caught my eye. One in particular was from the 2001 pile. It turned out to be a memo notifying us of someone's decision to change careers. I remember it basically said that after much consideration, an experienced staff member was resigning after 14 years of dedicated service, and that our new account representative would soon be in touch.

After further inspection, this letter took on more significance as I noted the address of the company: One World Trade Center, New York. The letter was dated sometime in May of 2001, only four months before September the 11th. I was so taken with the memo that I showed it to a fellow co-worker. It turns out that the pile of memos from 2001 was sprinkled with many letters from that same firm. I later learned that some staff members lost their lives, and some had survived. After pondering what had happened to us only hours ago, I reflected on how our lives can turn on one decision, one thought, one moment.

And still I (high) rise, even though some of my friends often say, "I couldn't work that high up…I don't see how you do it." Yet, I am ever mindful that my Lord is everywhere I am. He promised to never forsake me or leave me. That means that even if the day brings tragedy, I know I won't have to face it alone. So every workday, I continue to ascend, just a little closer to heaven, safe in His arms.

CHAPTER SEVEN

Harvest Of Plenty

I can still remember the many Sunday afternoon family dinners we had after church when I was young. It was always, and still is, a very precious time. I served as the official table-setter and "taste-tester," making sure everything was just right, and believe me it was!

No matter what meals were consumed during the week, Sunday dinner was extra special. Momma would always start the night before, cleaning greens, peeling fresh ears of corn, shelling field peas, steaming sweet potatoes, making cakes and fresh yeast rolls. She seemed to really get a joy from it all.

Nurturing is just her wonderful way of showing how much she loves us.

My mom not only had years of experience cooking for us, but she is from a family of eleven brothers and sisters who always seemed to have a feast for one reason or another. In addition, her master's degree in arts and education, with a concentration in home economics, didn't hurt her skills either.

And so it is to this day, that whenever my mom cooks, family and friends surround her to enjoy good food and have fun just being together. I guess nurturing is just her wonderful way of showing how much she loves us.

God yearns to nurture you.

God, too, yearns to nurture you. He wants to "sup" with you, sit and talk with you, and let you know just how much He loves you. God has prepared a table for you, and now He wants you to come and be fed. He knows you are hungry and in need. He knows what your spirit is longing for, so He has planned a special meal. This meal is one that He hopes you will consume, as it was prepared with you in mind. The invitation is now being extended to you. Now, the question becomes, will you take the time…make the time…to feast with the Master?

"Hey Kids…Supper's Ready"

Luke, chapter 14, speaks of various parables Jesus taught during a meal that He was invited to attend. As always, Jesus was teaching about righteous living. Beginning in verse 16, He begins telling the parable of The Great Dinner.

"Someone gave a great dinner and invited many. At the time for the dinner, he sent his slave to say to those who had been invited, 'Come; for everything is ready now'. My friend, God is calling you to Supper. He wants you to know that your invitation is still open, your place is set, and your dinner is waiting, still warm on the stove. And, what a feast He has planned for you!

My friend, God is calling you to Supper.

After accepting your invitation, you will be greeted with a Holy Kiss (II Corinthians 13:12). You will then be cleaned up and given the Best Robe (Luke 15:22). Your meal will begin with the Fruit of the Spirit (Galatians 5:22). The main course consists of Enduring Meat (St. John

6:27) and the True Bread (St. John 6:32-33). Your thirst will be quenched with Spring Water (St. John 4:14), and dessert will be Sweeter than Honey (Psalms 119:103). Such a wonderful meal deserves your attention! So ask yourself, what's your excuse for not showing up?

Such a wonderful meal deserves your attention!

The parable goes on to say: "*But they all alike began to make excuses. The first said to him, 'I have bought a piece of land, and I must go out and see it; please accept my regrets.' Another said, 'I have bought five yoke of oxen, and I am going to try them out; please accept my regrets.' Another said, 'I have just been married, and therefore I cannot come.'*

So the slave returned and reported this to his master. The owner of the house became angry and said to his slave, 'Go out at once into the streets and lanes of the town and bring in the poor, the crippled, the blind and the lame.' And the slave said, 'Sir, what you ordered has been done, and there is still room.' Then the master said to the slave, 'Go out into the roads and lanes, and compel people to come in, so that my house may be filled. For I tell you, none of those who were invited will taste my dinner."

Can you imagine standing up an invitation to dinner at the home of your city's most prominent citizen…or worse yet, missing an opportunity to have dinner with the president and first lady at the White House? *No Way*! Yet, how often do we miss the opportunity to dine at the Potter's House! (Jeremiah 18:1-6).

My friends, please know this one truth: *There are no understudies in this Christian life. Basically, if you're not where God wants you to be, "your spot is empty!*" So next time your invitation is extended, don't hesitate for one moment…*Go!*

It's Always Good

On a recent trip home, I accompanied my mom to a very unique restaurant located in a neighborhood called Germantown. This restaurant is famous for its family-style meals and down-home atmosphere. Upon entering the restaurant, I was immediately impressed with the 18th century decor, the eclectic blend of spring flowers and cornbread in the air, and the warm friendly greetings from the wait staff.

As we approached the entrance to the main dining room, we were asked if we had dined there before. I hadn't, but my mom had. So the waiter turned to me and said, "Well, it's simple; you just sit where I tell you and eat what I give you." I openly giggled, admiring his humor. However, I soon learned that his humor served to buffer the truth…he was not kidding. All restaurant patrons were seated alike, in locations determined by the wait staff, at huge dining room tables that easily sat twelve people. The tables were already set with china and stemware, fruit tea, ice-cold water, and dessert…that day it was double chocolate cake.

Once seated, a waitress began to bring to our table large bowls filled with delicious food we were instructed to share. We never knew what was coming until it arrived, but it was *always good*. That day, we feasted on three kinds of salad, eight vegetables, three meats, homemade rolls and cornbread. We were all encouraged to eat until we were satisfied, and believe me we were. I would never have guessed that a restaurant that doesn't let guests decide what they want would rarely have a dissatisfied customer! So, if you ever have the chance to visit Germantown in Nashville, Tennessee, be sure to eat at Monell's. I promise you won't be disappointed. In fact, when most people just *hear* about this place, *they go*, sight unseen. Now just think, if one can trust a complete stranger about a restaurant, why not trust the Master and accept his open invitation to sup with Him? So please don't hesitate any more…*just go!*

Facing The Facts

Now granted, I know first-hand that this "go" thing is not easy. If you're like me, an awful lot of areas in my life need "growing up" before I can "go." The fact is, I am more-often-than-not so self-absorbed by my earthly reasons for "not making time to come to supper with Christ" that I fail to see my true spiritual identity.

Then one day, I stumbled across a scripture in Ephesians 3:19 saying,…*"to know the love of Christ that surpasses knowledge, so that you may be filled with all the fullness of God."* That scripture spoke to me that the Love of God is able to surpass my knowledge…whatever I know to be a fact *pales* to the power of God's *true love.(The Truth)*.

In other words, God's truth is more powerful than the facts… AWESOME! So, when faced with the awful facts of your life, think on the awesome truth of God!

Your Facts	His Truth	His Word
Poor	Rich	II Corinth. 9:11-12
Wanting	Satisfied	Psalms 63:5
Afraid	Bold	Matthew 17:7-8
Unqualified	Favored	Proverbs 8:35
Sick	Healed	Luke 6:19
Anxious	Confident	Hebrews 10:35-36
Outcast	Reconciled	II Corinth. 6:17-18

Take time to look up these scriptures and continuously meditate on them, for the scripture says in St. John 8:32 that…*"ye shall know the*

Truth (His Word), *and the Truth will make you free"* (from being negatively influenced by your facts)!

Oh, my brothers and sisters, when you finally realize the power of God's Truth as found in *The Word*, only then will all your blessings begin to pour through the windows (Malachi 3:10)! And the good news is, God has them all waiting for you, just *waiting until you are ready to receive them!*

And so we end as we began, with *The Word*.

My dear friend, *now* is the time to gather unto yourself the blessings He has so sweetly ripened for you in *The Word: Blessings of Peace, Freedom, Fruit-Filled Living, Stewardship, Assurance, Wisdom, Daily Benefits, and Prospering Health are now ready for you to harvest*. And what a sweet harvest it is! *"Oh, Taste and See that the Lord is Good! Blessed is the man that trusts in Him."* (Psalm 34:8). So come on! What are you waiting for? Now is *not* the time to give up, but to get into *The Word*...now is your time...It's Harvest Time!

Jewel: Galatians 6:9
Let us not become weary in doing good, for at the proper time, we will reap a harvest if we do not give up.

Notes

Notes

0-595-28113-3